Roman Catholicism:

An Introduction and Bible Study

Thomas P. Johnston, Ph.D.

(1/27/26 1:26 PM).

Evangelism Unlimited, Inc.
Bemimdji, MN
2026

The purpose of this booklet is to understanding Roman Catholicism especially in comparison with contemporary Evangelicalism. The effort may appear overly ambitious as the task is enormous. Western church history covers two millennia of church and state interrelationships, as well as doctrinal and military conflicts spanning numerous languages, cultures, and socio-economic classes. Western church history also boasts an enormous loss of life (especially in the second millennium) along with constant doctrinal innovation and development. The topic is pretentious. The challenge daunting.

In 2025 the *Osservatore Romano*, Rome's weekly newspaper was published in 85 languages. At least 85 language groups today treasure their church history that includes Roman Catholicism at some level. Fluency in only a handful of languages cannot provide the depth of understanding necessary to grasp all the contexts of such a vast subject, or can it?

Can main lines of consideration be found to provide the earnest reader an introductory point of view of Roman Catholicism? With soberness of mind, this author seeks to provide lines of thought to assist the noble reader in understanding Roman Catholicism in the North American context. The final portion of this paper is given to reflection points with a focus on Holy Scripture. The Bible verses are meant to suggest biblical topics and themes to challenge common doctrinal or practical divergences in Catholicism. The goal is for the esteemed reader to consider the complex subject of "What is Roman Catholicism in comparison to modern Evangelicalism?" We begin with an introduction to the development of the state-church structure.

Rome's First Millennium

Before Constantine it is difficult to conceive the church as a department of the state, or the state as a department of the church. Constantine lived from 272-337 A.D. He took three decisive actions that proved seminal in the development of the Catholic hegemony.

Contantine was the first Roman emperor to convert to Christianity, even though he was not baptized until his deathbed. In 315 A.D., in his oft recounted "conversion" experience, Constantine had a vision of a cross in the sky bearing the inscription, *In Hoc Signo Vinces* ("In this sign thou shalt conquer"). Constantine apparently took this vision to mean that he should leverage Christianity to achieve his political and military goals. Christianity became tool for him to grow the size, power, and stability of the

Roman Empire. From that point on, Christianity and political power commingled within the Roman Empire.

Constantine's vision of a state church led to his second decisive action. Since political entities tend to regulate everything they touch, roads, schools, and businesses, Rome needed a way to regulate its newly acquired church. It did so by regulating doctrine. In 325 A.D. Constantine called together the Council of Nicaea. The result of this council was the formulation of the Nicene Creed. The Nicene Creed then became the litmus test for who is "in" and who is "not in" the approved state church. Whether or not the Nicene Creed was successful in keeping the church firmly founded on the teachings of Jesus in the Scriptures is a topic for another paper. From that point on, Rome's political and ecclesiastical machinery began increasingly regulating doctrine, and soon matters of church practice throughout the Western Empire.

A third consequential decision of Constantine was moving the capital city of the Roman Empire. In 330 A.D., Constantine moved the Roman Empire's capital city 1,386 miles east (by current land routes), from Rome (Italy) to Byzantium (Istanbul, Turkey). This decision led to the formation of two dominant cultures and language groups within this state church, one Greek-speaking and the other Latin-speaking. Both poles of the Roman Empire remained united for about 300 years. That is, the same Roman emperor ruled both the Greek and Latin portions of the empire. However, in 602 A.D., Emperor Maurice was assassinated in Constantinople. Maurice was the last Roman emperor to rule over both Byzantium and Rome. From that time on Europe divided into two empires, Eastern Europe and Western Europe. They were different in language, culture, and religion. Rome's monopoly over the church was split into two pieces. Yet Rome's regulatory machine kept churning in the Latin-speaking side of Europe.

Augustine of Hippo (354-430 A.D.) became a champion of Rome's regulatory machine. He began as a promising lawyer in Milan and became the bishop of Hippo in 395 A.D. four years after his ordination as a priest. His skills as a debater and his commitment as an apologist for Rome earned him the post in the city of Hippo in north Africa. He was sent there to counter the dissenting Donatists of that area—Hippo was about 105 miles from Carthage, the seat of the Donatists. These Latin-speaking Donatists dissented from Rome in matters of doctrine and practice. Augustine applied his voice and pen in politicking and writing against the Donatists, as well as other dissenters from the state church. Gleaning arguments from anti-heresy authors before him, he wrote against the heretics of his day. Augustine wrote against the Manicheans and the Donatists. He also penned arguments against his freewill rival Pelagius.

As may be ascertained, Augustine's arguments are not for the feeble of mind. This author wonders if he went beyond Scripture in accusing others. In *Contra Donatisten* (Against the Donatists), Augustine argued against those in north Africa who would dare to defy the bishop of Rome and his teachings on the Sacraments. With *Contra Manichean* (Against the Manicheans), using the fallacy of composition Augustine conflated believers in spiritual rebirth with the dualism of a certain Manichaeus. In *Contra Pelagius*, any evangelist who called his hearers to repentance and prayer before they are water baptized was deemed to deny the doctrine of original sin. For this author, Augustine's pen sowed discord into the household of God, while likewise arming enemies of the biblical gospel of salvation.

Because of his great mind and many writings Augustine has become a historical and theological touchstone. His scholarship was so prominent that he was quoted by Luther and Calvin. He was also quoted by proponents of the sacramental church. On one hand he spoke masterfully on certain issues—such as the sovereignty of God—on the other hand he spoke against a freedom of conscience when it was poised against Rome.

Augustine was a master of debater. He remains the intellectual hero of the first millennium for the sacramental Church of Rome. For example, 700 years after his death, Augustine was the most often cited ancient "Father" (or theologian) by Peter the Lombard in his 1160 A.D. *Four Books of Sentences*. Lombard's translator from Latin into English wrote, "It can be said with some justification that nine-tenths of the [Lombard] *Sentences* consist of Augustinian texts."[1] In his 1265 A.D. *Summa Theologica*, written almost 850 years after the death of Augustine, 75% of his citations were sourced from Augustine. It is not possible to overstate the impact of Augustine's writings on the theology of the Church of Rome.

---

[1] Giulio Silano, "Introduction" in Peter Lombard, *The Sentences: Book 1, The Mystery of the Trinity*; trans. by Giulio Silano (Toronto: PIMS, 2007), xxvii.

As it turns out, Augustine's *cause célèbre* occurred when a Donatist rebaptized a previously baptized Catholic. The temerity of that Donatist to rebaptize a Catholic confronted Augustine's own sacramental view of Baptism. After arguments failed to change the thinking and practice of this Donatist, Augustine resorted to the use of political force. In his position as personal priest to the King of Hippo, Augustine counseled him and also wrote letters to other political leaders, admonishing them in their oversight of religious affairs. There was no separation of church and state in those days. In Augustine's letters to Bonifacius, the Roman Count of Africa under Valentinian III, Augustine prescribed the use of political force to bend the Donatists to submit to the doctrines and practices of Rome. The religious dominance urged by Augustine to force their submission included the imposition of fines, corporeal punishment, and imprisonment.

Several centuries after Augustine, Pope Gregory I (590-604 A.D.) reiterated the precedent set by Augustine. He wrote instructions regarding the Donatists to Gennadius (Patrician and Exarch of Africa), to Gaudiosus (the Master of the African Militia), and to all the Catholic bishops of Africa. Gregory called for various levels of political persecution against these dissenting Christians of his time. Both Augustine and Gregory set a precedent for the crusades and inquisitions that were to dominate Western Europe in the twelfth and thirteenth centuries.

Building from this framework of Augustinianism, the Second Council of Orange (529 A.D) scuttled the evangelism efforts of travelling evangelists in the early Middle Ages. While a blanket of spiritual darkness fell upon Western Christianity, these "Wandering Preachers" (*Wanderprediger*) continued to share the gospel. God did not leave Himself without a witness (Acts 14:17). While few writings of these medieval revivalists and evangelists have survived, their teachings and success can be deduced by the writings against them. It can be ascertained that the gospel went out in boldness and truth in diverse regions and at varied times. Even so, early in the second millennium two decisive events set the path for the modern Church of Rome.

Rome's Second Millennium

Two important events set the tracts upon which Roman Catholicism has traveled: the Great Schism and Lombard's *Four Books of Sentences*. Properly calibrating the importance of these events provides a better understanding of the Church of Rome's place in the modern world. The first event was the Great Schism of 1054 A.D. This mutual anathema formally divided the state church founded by Constantine into two state church groupings. The branch headquartered in Rome was Latin speaking. This Latin church was highly centralized. It took the name "catholic"—meaning "universal." The second branch from this split was Greek speaking. Its central base was in Constantinople or Byzantium (Istanbul, Turkey). It took the name "orthodox" to highlight its focus on "right doctrine." Byzantium had a more regionalized system of government. Its many cooperating churches were *auto-cephalous*, meaning that each church had independent "headship." Major language groups had their own bishop, patriarch, or pope who oversaw the doctrine and practice of the church in their region and language group.

Consider, for example, the six churches currently sharing the Church of the Holy Sepulchre in Jerusalem today are Orthodox. They churches are: Greek Orthodox, Latins (Roman Catholic), Armenian Orthodox, Egyptian Coptic, Syriac Orthodox, and Ethiopian Orthodox.[i] Five are *auto-cephalous* Orthodox churches, differentiated by the language in their name. Not included among these churches are other Orthodox churches in other language groups, such as Russian Orthodox, Bulgarian Orthodox, Ukrainian Orthodox, Georgian Orthodox, Chinese Orthodox, Korean Orthodox, and the Orthodox Church in American. Therefore, since 1054 A.D. it is quite impossible that the Roman Catholic church should consider itself truly catholic or "universal," even while this goal appears to be its aspiration. Rome has never been the universal church.

Meanwhile, Rome still operates like the Roman Empire. It maintains a centralized government poised to influence countries under its sway by sending priests and bishops to act as ambassadors to the political leaders (kings, queens, and princes), as well as to important religious figures. Rome remains structured as an empire overseeing vice regents (kings and kingdoms) under its spiritual and political oversight. However, just as the Catholic Church flourishes under a state-church model, Orthodox churches often enjoy close relationships with the political systems in their language group.

Quite apart from these two state-churches, other independent, free, or dissenting churches existed in the first millennium and a half before the Protestant Reformation. They have been called by diverse titles in various areas, often named by their antagonists. Before 1054 A.D. there were the Montanists, Monarchists, Novatians, Nestorians, Donatists, Paulicians, and Bogomiles. After 1054 A.D. and prior to 1517 A.D. (the dawn of the Protestant Reformation) non-state-church assemblies also existed. They are described by the following names: Petrobusians, Henricians, Cathars, Waldensians, Albigensians, Wycliffites, and Hussites. Their inclusion in these lists does not indicate an endorsement nor does it imply that their beliefs were common among them or consistent over time. Their existence merely exemplifies that Rome was never the universal church even in Medieval Western Europe. Additionally, there is strong evidence that Sabbatarians and Pentecostals existed since the earlier times. It appears that the seven churches described in Revelation 2-3 continue to exist in every age of the church and in every culture where a church has been planted. Meanwhile it remains a mystery to classify most churches using the typology established in the seven churches of Revelation.

With its regulating reflex, the Church of Rome soon became an adversary of these dissident groups. Once it controlled the political system in an area through winning the military crusades, then it could apply a centralized religious governance as taught in Deuteronomy 17. Next Rome used inquisition techniques taught in Deuteronomy 13 to ferret out and crush any non-conforming religious groups. Finally, once it controlled historians and the printing presses, Rome erased the memory of these dissident churches from under heaven. They applied the teaching of Deuteronomy 25:

> "**Therefore it shall come about when the LORD your God has given you rest from all your surrounding enemies, in the land which the LORD your God gives you as an inheritance to possess, you shall blot out the memory of Amalek from under heaven; you must not forget**" (Deut. 25:19 NASB).

The splitting of Constantine's state-church model into two groups of churches early in the second millennium continues to contradict Rome's claim to universality. Then, a second major event took place in the twelfth century. The occasion was the first formulation of Rome's sacramental system as the Seven Sacraments.

The Seven Sacraments of the Church

The second major event in the early second millennium was the doctrinal shift that took place in the Church of Rome 1100 years into its existence. Under the influence of Bernard of Clairvaux (1090-1153 A.D.) Rome more narrowly defined its doctrine and practice. Clairvaux became patron for Peter Lombard (1096-1160 A.D.), who is also known as Master Peter. In 1134 A.D. Clairvaux sent a letter to Hugh, Abbot of Saint Victor in Paris. In his letter, Clairvaux introduced Lombard to Hugh and strongly urged his patronage of Lombard, that is, allow Lombard to reside at the Abbey of Saint Victor. Hugh accepted Clairvaux's request. Later in 1140-1141 A.D. Lombard attended the Council of Sens with Clairvaux. Sens is a city located 125 kilometers or 78 miles southeast of Paris. This council resulted in the condemnation of Peter Abelard as a heretic. Abelard is best known for his secret marriage to Eloise of Argenteuil. Abelard taught that celibacy should be a discipline, but not a dogma. On the other hand, Clairvaux strongly defended clerical celibacy as necessary dogma. Clairvaux championed the Sacrament of Holy Orders requiring priests and monks to take a vow of celibacy. Agreeing with Clairvaux, Lombard argued a unique form of allegorical interpretation for the cause of priestly celibacy. Abelard lost the debate in Sens. The force of Lombard's logic validated Clairvaux' patronage. Master Peter went on to author his *Four Books of Sentences*[2] teaching his unique brand of allegorical interpretation.[3] These four books became the foundation for all Roman Catholic theological training for over 300 years.[4]

---

[2]"Church of the Holy Sepulchre chapels"; available at: https://www.seetheholyland.net/church-of-the-holy-sepulchre-chapels/ (Online); accessed 14 Nov 2025; Internet.

[3]My paper, "The Holy Spirit's work" is available at https://www.nobts.edu/baptist-center-theology/journals/journals/JBTM_16-2_Fall_2019.pdf (Online); accessed: 14 Nov 2025; Internet, as well as at https://www.evangelismunlimited.org/c/papers (Online); accessed: 14 Nov 2025; Internet.

[4]"...The Four Books of Sentences became, on the recommendation of the Lateran Council (1215), the foundational manual for theology in the universities from the thirteenth to fifteenth centuries" (Mark Ozilou, *Pierre Lombard: Les Quatres Livres de Sentences, Livre Premier* [Paris: Cerf, 2012], back cover; translation mine).

During his three decades at Saint Victor, Lombard taught through, revised, and completed his *Four Books of Sentences*. He ended his career as the bishop of Paris. His *Four Books* were used as a two-year course of theological study. In two years, a student would be immersed in medieval Catholic thought. In addition, these *Four Books* of Master Peter became the basis for the modern master's degree—a foundation stone in establishing Catholic universities across Europe. The first three of these *Four Books* explained Lombard's allegorical interpretation of the Bible, paving the way for Book Four on the Seven Sacraments. These four volumes cemented the Seven Sacraments as the basis for salvation in Roman Catholicism. In the next century, Pope Innocent III added his *imprimatur* (his stamp) to Lombard's *Four Books*. At the Fourth Lateran Council of 1215 A.D. it was decreed that no Catholic theologian could write negatively of Lombard and his *Four Books of Sentences.*

Available only in Latin for 850 years, these *Four Books* have only very recently become fully available in English.[5] Their exclusivity in Latin sheltered them from regular Evangelical scrutiny. It might shock the reader to know that the Seven Sacraments were never universally taught or accepted in the Church of Rome for its first 1100 years. It was not until the Council of Trent (1545-1560 A.D.)—400 years after Lombard—that they were formally adopted by a council of the Church of Rome. This fact alone provides another counter to Rome's argument for the unchanging constancy of its views.

It is important to understand the impregnable autocratic force by which Lombard's *Four Books* were utilized. For 300 years (a third of a millennium) Western European universities required two years of study of, teaching from, writing on, and affirmation of Lombard's *Four Books of Sentences* for a master's in theology and to teach theology. During those same 300 years, these theology students were not allowed to read a Bible in Latin or in their own language. For 300 years before the Protestant Reformation, all doctrinal questions were framed in, with, and by Lombard's allegorical interpretative and sacramental system. Lombard codified what was truly Catholic. When Martin Luther and

---

[5]Peter Lombard, *The Sentences: Book 1, The Mystery of the Trinity*; trans. by Giulio Silano (Toronto: PIMS, 2007); *The Sentences: Book 2, On Creation*; trans. by Giulio Silano (Toronto: PIMS, 2008); The Sentences: *Book 3, On the Incarnation of the Word*; trans. by Giulio Silano (Toronto: PIMS, 2008); The Sentences: *Book 4, On the Doctrine of Signs*; trans. by Giulio Silano (Toronto: PIMS, 2010).

John Calvin separated from the Church of Rome, they separated from Lombard's sacramental and interpretive system.

As a result of Lombard's views—and those of many others after him who further redefined and refined his ideas—biblical Christianity and Roman Catholicism became two vastly different systems of thought. By the sixteenth century, the Protestant Reformation under Luther and Calvin called attention to the immense doctrinal and practical differences between these two religious systems.

The basis for Sacramentalism is as follows. In Catholicism the Holy Spirit operates and limits His saving effects through inhabiting physical objects, such as water, bread, and oil. According to the Catholic system, the right words uttered over these physical objects by a rightly approved priest call down the real presence of the Holy Spirit within that object. It follows then that the spirit-infused object accomplishes the spiritual effect it is purposed to fulfill. In Catholicism, the sacramental objects become true receptacles of the Holy Spirit to accomplish His work in, with, and by these objects. Hence, in Catholicism, the ministry of the Holy Spirit is limited to His effects through the physical objects of the Sacraments.

Evangelicalism is wholly other. In Evangelicalism the saving effects of the Holy Spirit come through the impact of the words of the Bible on the hearts, minds, and souls of men.[6] These words lead to repentance and faith in some,[7] and hardness of heart in

---

[6] "Over against this whole view evangelicalism, seeking to conserve what it conceives to be only consistent supernaturalism, sweeps away every intermediary between the soul and its God, and leaves the soul dependent for its salvation on God alone, operating upon it by his immediate grace. … That only is true evangelicalism, therefore, in which sounds clearly the double confession that all the power exerted in saving the soul is from God, and that God in his saving operations acts directly upon the soul." (B. B. Warfield, The Plan of *Salvation* [1918]; available at: https://www.monergism.com/thethreshold/sdg/pdf/warfield_plan.pdf (Online); accessed: 29 Oct 2025; Internet).

[7] "Teachers are, in their turn, admonished to beware of bringing forward anything but the pure word of God, for if this was not allowable for Paul, it will not be so for any one in the present day. He proves, however, from the effect produced, that it was the word of God that he had delivered, inasmuch as it had produced that fruit of heavenly doctrine which the Prophets celebrate, (Isaiah 55:11; Jeremiah 23:29) in renewing their life, for the doctrine of men could accomplish no such thing." (*Calvin's Commentary on 1 Thessalonians 2:13*; available at:

others.[8] The only intermediary in Evangelicalism is the still small voice of the Holy Spirit speaking in, with, and by the words of the Word of God through reading or by the mouth of an evangelist or preacher—this is the original basis for the term Evangelical. The Holy Spirit Himself acts directly upon the souls of men.[9] Salvation is enacted upon the soul in this order:

1. Hearing the words of the gospel from Scripture (1 Thess. 2:13).
2. That hearing resulting in faith within some (Rom. 10:17).
3. That hearing of faith is fully provided by the grace of God alone (Eph. 2:8-9).
4. These things happen because of the atoning work of Christ on the cross (Isa. 53:5-6).

To observe all these steps described in one place, please see Acts 15:7-11 and Romans 3:19-26.

In Catholicism it's all about physical species and includes many intermediaries. In biblical Evangelicalism there are no physical species for salvation. For Evangelicals physical species and many intermediaries represent dangerous additions to the biblical gospel. Furthermore, the Book of Galatians teaches that false teaching does not remain passive and innocuous. False teaching foments like gangrene, poisoning all other doctrines. The Apostle Paul explained this ruinous phenomenon, "**A little leaven leavens the whole lump**" (Gal. 5:9 ESV).

---

https://www.studylight.org/commentaries/eng/cal/1-thessalonians-2.html [Online]; accessed 29 Oct 2025; Internet).

[8]"It indeed appears evident, that the word of God is not equally efficacious in all. ... Nothing of this kind is found in the reprobate; for they either carelessly disregard God speaking to them, and thus mock him, or clamour against his truth, and obstinately resist it." (*Calvin's Commentary on Hebrews 4:12*; available at: https://www.studylight.org/commentaries/eng/cal/hebrews-4.html [Online]; accessed 29 Oct 2025; Internet).

[9]"As we have said, God never has dealt, and never does deal, with mankind at any time otherwise than by the word of promise. Neither can we, on our part, ever have to do with God otherwise than through faith in His word and promise." (Martin Luther, "The Pagan Servitude of the Church," in *Martin Luther: Selections from His Writings Edited and with Introduction*, John Dillenberger, ed. [Garden City, NY: Doubleday, 1961], 277).

Whereas in its first millennium Rome advanced its state-church interconnectivity, in the second millennium Rome formalized a doctrinal system that buttressed its universalistic instinct. With its Seven Sacraments Rome was now poised to remain the sole universal church. Pragmatism enacted its toll on biblical faithfulness. From this author's point-of-view, the Bible debunks some key teachings of the Roman Catholic Church.

Looking at the Scripture

From a Baptist point of view, Evangelical converts to Catholicism will face a series of doctrinal and practical compromises. These divergencies will become evident as they attend Mass at a Catholic church or cathedral. The accommodations may appear trivial at first. But they comprise a larger system of teaching, infecting the whole lump. Even the smallest false teaching represents an active doctrinal virus multiplying deviations from biblical Christianity and the plain reading of the biblical text.

The remainder of this booklet is designed for individual and small group Bible study. Its content is gathered to engage those interested in Catholicism with issues they will encounter when attending a Catholic church. Each sample divergency is followed by several Scripture passages that address the topic in question. This list of false teachings is not designed to be exhaustive. The topics do not contain sample citations from Catholic resources. Books explaining Roman Catholic teachings are readily available.[10] It

---

[10] James McCarthy, *The Gospel According to Rome: Comparing Catholic Tradition and the Word of God*; Foreword by John MacArthur (Eugene, OR: Harvest House, 1995); Lorraine Boettner, *Roman Catholicism* (Phillipsburg, NJ: Presbyterian and Reformed, 1962); Gregg Allison, *40 Questions about Roman Catholicism* (Grand Rapids: Kregel, 2021); Leonardo de Chirico, *A Christian's Pocket Guide to Papacy: Its origin and role in the 21st Century* (Fearn, Ross-Shire, Scotland: Christian Focus, 2015), *A Christian's Pocket Guide to Mary: Mother of God?* (Fearn, Ross-Shire, Scotland: Christian Focus, 2017), and *Same Words, Different Worlds: Do Roman Catholics and Evangelicals Believe the Same Gospel?* (London: Inter-Varsity Press, 2021); and in French: Jacques Blocher, *Le Catholicisme à la lumière de l'Écriture Sainte*, 3rd edition (Nogent-sur-Marne, France: Éditions de l'Institut Biblique, 1979). Consider also these two chronological studies supported with Scripture and Catholic primary resources: Thomas P. Johnston, "Timelines for Western Christianity": Vol 1, *Chronological Theology* and Vol 2, *Geographic History* (Liberty, MO: Evangelism Unlimited, 2016).

is this author's prayer that the dear reader will consider the false teachings one by one, meditate upon the Scriptures listed, and ask God for clarity on each of these points.

1. Prayer to Mary and the saints:

   "**Pray, then, in this way: 'Our Father who is in heaven, Hallowed be Your name**'" (Matt. 6:9 NASB).

   "**In that day you will ask nothing of me. Truly, truly, I say to you, whatever you ask of the Father in my name, he will give it to you. Until now you have asked nothing in my name. Ask, and you will receive, that your joy may be full**" (John 16:23-24 ESV).

   "**And there is salvation in no one else, for there is no other name under heaven given among men by which we must be saved**" (Acts 4:12 ESV).

   There is no other name under heaven given among men but the name of Jesus. Prayer is to be made to God the Father, in the name of Jesus. This excludes all prayer in the name of the Holy Trinity or Mary, or prayer to any saint, angel, or dead relative.

2. Worship of physical objects, such as bowing to the Host (bread of the Eucharist), kissing the altar at the front of the church, or bowing before, praying to, and kissing any statue:

   "**You shall not make for yourself an idol, or any likeness of what is in heaven above or on the earth beneath or in the water under the earth. You shall not worship them or serve them; for I, the LORD your God, am a jealous God, visiting the iniquity of the fathers on the children, and on the third and the fourth generations of those who hate Me, but showing lovingkindness to thousands, to those who love Me and keep My commandments**" (Deut. 5:8-10 NASB).

   "**Then the LORD spoke to you from the midst of the fire; you heard the sound of words, but you saw no form — only a voice. ... So watch yourselves carefully, since you did not see any form on the day the LORD spoke to you at Horeb**

from the midst of the fire, so that you do not act corruptly and make a graven image for yourselves in the form of any figure, the likeness of male or female, the likeness of any animal that is on the earth, the likeness of any winged bird that flies in the sky, the likeness of anything that creeps on the ground, the likeness of any fish that is in the water below the earth. And beware not to lift up your eyes to heaven and see the sun and the moon and the stars, all the host of heaven, band be drawn away and worship them and serve them, those which the LORD your God has allotted to all the peoples under the whole heaven" (Deut. 4:12, 15-19 NASB).

The worship of created things is also addressed by Paul in Romans 1:23. God was sure that He did not reveal a form of Himself as described by Moses in Deuteronomy 4. Nevertheless, Aaron, the brother of Moses, made a golden calf for the people to worship (see Exodus 32). This golden calf was great sin. Likewise we need to watch out lest we substitute the worship of anything other than God who has communicated to us through His words.

3. Worshipping the "Host" or the bread of the Lord's Supper:

"He removed the high places and broke down the sacred pillars and cut down the Asherah. He also broke in pieces the bronze serpent that Moses had made, for until those days the sons of Israel burned incense to it; and it was called Nehushtan" (2 Kings 18:4 NASB).

"The children gather wood, and the fathers kindle the fire, and the women knead dough to make cakes for the queen of heaven; and they pour out drink offerings to other gods in order to spite Me" (Jer. 7:18 NASB).

"**Because they exchanged the truth about God for a lie and worshiped and served the creature rather than the Creator, who is blessed forever! Amen**" (Rom. 1:25 ESV).

Just as the people of Israel falsely worshiped physical objects, it is dangerous to confuse God's use of objects with the worship of God Himself. God forbids the worship of created things (physical objects).

4. Worshipping angels:

"For to which of the angels did God ever say, 'You are my Son, today I have begotten you'?" (Heb. 1:5 ESV).

There is a danger of exchanging the worship that belongs only to Jesus with the worship of angelic beings. Rather than worship angels, we need to understand their role:

"Now I, John, saw and heard these things. And when I heard and saw, I fell down to worship before the feet of the angel who showed me these things. Then he said to me, 'See that you do not do that. For I am your fellow servant, and of your brethren the prophets, and of those who keep the words of this book. Worship God'" (Rev. 22:8-9 NKJV). Also consider Revelation 19:9-10 for deeper study and reflection.

We must obey the teaching of these angels to the Apostle John. John was forbidden from bowing down or worshipping the angels who were standing right before him. Likewise, it is dangerous for us to replace the worship of God with angels.

5. The acknowledgement of many intermediaries, such as Mary and priests, and the saints:

"For there is one God and one Mediator between God and men, the Man Christ Jesus, who gave Himself a ransom for all, to be testified in due time, for which I was appointed a preacher and an apostle—I am speaking the truth in Christ and not lying—a teacher of the Gentiles in faith and truth" (1 Tim. 2:5-7 NKJV).

Christ and Christ alone is our Lawyer, Advocate, and Mediator. Apart from Him there is no other:

"My little children, I am writing these things to you so that you may not sin. But if anyone does sin, we have an advocate with the Father, Jesus Christ the righteous. He is the propitiation for our sins, and not for ours only but also for the sins of the whole world" (1 John 2:1-2 ESV).

Jesus Christ alone is worthy of praise, honor, and glory:

"And I saw in the right hand of Him who sat on the throne a scroll written inside and on the back, sealed with seven seals. Then I saw a strong angel proclaiming with a loud voice, 'Who is worthy to open the scroll and to loose its seals?' And no one in heaven or on the earth or under the earth was able to open the scroll, or to look at it. So I wept much, because no one was found worthy to open and read the scroll, or to look at it. But one of the elders said to me, 'Do not weep. Behold, the Lion of the tribe of Judah, the Root of David, has prevailed to open the scroll and to loose its seven seals'" (Rev. 5:1-5 NKJV).

Christ alone is worthy, and to Christ alone belongs all the glory, because He has redeemed us by His blood:

"And they sang a new song, saying: 'You are worthy to take the scroll, and to open its seals; for You were slain, and have redeemed us to God by Your blood out of every tribe and tongue and people and nation, and have made us kings and priests to our God; and we shall reign on the earth'" (Rev. 5:9-10 NKJV).

"Then I looked, and I heard around the throne and the living creatures and the elders the voice of many angels, numbering myriads of myriads and thousands of thousands, saying with a loud voice, 'Worthy is the Lamb who was slain, to receive power and wealth and wisdom and might and honor and glory and blessing!'" (Rev. 5:11-12 ESV).

There is a very real danger in inserting spiritual intermediaries when and where the Bible does not specifically authorize us to do so.

6. The canonizing of saints:

Regarding the regular canonizing of saints by the Catholic Church: only Jesus Christ has the power to sanctify (make holy, or make into a saint), and He Himself makes us holy by His Holy Spirit:

"**Or do you not know that the unrighteous will not inherit the kingdom of God? Do not be deceived: neither the sexually immoral, nor idolaters, nor adulterers, nor men who practice homosexuality, nor thieves, nor the greedy, nor drunkards, nor revilers, nor swindlers will inherit the kingdom of God. And such were some of you. But you were washed, you were sanctified, you were justified in the name of the Lord Jesus Christ and by the Spirit of our God**" (1 Cor. 6:9-11 ESV).

"**And by that will we have been sanctified through the offering of the body of Jesus Christ once for all**" (Heb. 10:10 ESV).

It is Jesus who determines who is holy and who is not. No one on earth is given that power or authority. Jesus makes holy (sanctifies) and Jesus determines who is holy.

7. Bowing before men:

"**And another angel, a third, followed them, saying with a loud voice, 'If anyone worships the beast and its image and receives a mark on his forehead or on his hand, he also will drink the wine of God's wrath, poured full strength into the cup of his anger, and he will be tormented with fire and sulfur in the presence of the holy angels and in the presence of the Lamb. And the smoke of their torment goes up forever and ever, and they have no rest, day or night, these worshipers of the beast and its image, and whoever receives the mark of its name**'" (Rev. 14:9-11 ESV).

One day the beast will require all people on earth to bow before him and worship him. However, the worship of men is forbidden in both the Old and New Testaments. In Daniel 3, Shadrach, Meshach, and Abed-Nego refused to bow before the golden image made by King Nebuchadnezzar. Although they were thrown into a fiery furnace, they survived without the smell of smoke. Nebuchadnezzar saw Jesus walking in the midst of the fire along with the three. God is very jealous of His worship, which is why we must not bow before men.

8. Calling someone on earth a spiritual "Father":

"But you, do not be called 'Rabbi'; for One is your Teacher, the Christ, and you are all brethren. Do not call anyone on earth your father; for One is your Father, He who is in heaven. And do not be called teachers; for One is your Teacher, the Christ" (Matt. 23:8-10 NKJV).

In obedience to the teaching of Jesus, we must take heed lest we give anyone on earth the religious title of "Father."

9. Deeding spiritual authority to men or obeying man above obeying Christ and His words:

Biblical Christians are called to follow only after Jesus Christ:

"And Jesus said to them, 'Follow Me, and I will make you become fishers of men'" (Mark 1:17 NASB). Also consider Mark 8:34-35 and John 14:6 for deeper study and reflection.

"And Jesus came up and spoke to them, saying, 'All authority has been given to Me in heaven and on earth'" (Matt. 28:18 NASB).

Jesus never deeded His authority to anyone else. And yes, obeying Christ comes at a cost. You will be hated and persecuted by worldly minded people:

"You will be hated by all because of My name, but it is the one who has endured to the end who will be saved" (Matt. 10:22 NASB). Also consider Matthew 24:9-13 on this topic.

Even so, only the words and commandments of Jesus are to be obeyed:

"Whoever has my commandments and keeps them, he it is who loves me. And he who loves me will be loved by my Father, and I will love him and manifest

myself to him" (John 14:21 ESV). Please also see Matthew 7:24-27 and Luke 6:46-49 where Jesus explained the importance of His very words.

10. Forced celibacy and regulated fast days:

"**Now the Spirit expressly says that in later times some will depart from the faith by devoting themselves to deceitful spirits and teachings of demons, through the insincerity of liars whose consciences are seared, who forbid marriage and require abstinence from foods that God created to be received with thanksgiving by those who believe and know the truth**" (1 Tim. 4:1-3 ESV). Paul also wrote some very helpful verses in Romans 14:1-6 encouraging his readers to avoid judgment and discord on petty issues.

Jesus Christ has called us and saved us to live in freedom, not under a yoke of petty regulations:

"**Therefore, if you died with Christ from the basic principles of the world, why, as though living in the world, do you subject yourselves to regulations—'Do not touch, do not taste, do not handle,' which all concern things which perish with the using—according to the commandments and doctrines of men? These things indeed have an appearance of wisdom in self-imposed religion, false humility, and neglect of the body, but are of no value against the indulgence of the flesh**" (Col. 2:20-23 NKJV).

For example, in the case of eating meat sacrificed to idols, Paul recommended freedom as well as the honor of the conscience of other Christians in 1 Corinthians 10:23-33.

11. "Voluntary Poverty" and the Vow of Celibacy:

"**Go; behold, I send you out as lambs in the midst of wolves. Carry no money belt, no bag, no shoes; and greet no one on the way**" (Luke 10:3-4 NASB).

"**And He said to them, 'When I sent you out without money belt and bag and sandals, you did not lack anything, did you?' They said, 'No, nothing.' And He said to them, 'But now, whoever has a money belt is to take it along, likewise**

also a bag; and whoever has no sword is to sell his coat and buy one'" (Luke 22:35-36 NASB).

Before His death and resurrection, Jesus sent out His disciples empty handed. But just prior to His death, Jesus changed this command, which is why in the Book of Acts the disciples owned homes and were married, just like Philip the evangelist:

"**On the next day we who were Paul's companions departed and came to Caesarea, and entered the house of Philip the evangelist, who was one of the seven, and stayed with him. Now this man had four virgin daughters who prophesied**" (Acts 21:8-9 NKJV).

On the other hand, the combining of resources with others (to live in a commune) can be used by the wicked to lure the naïve into their evil lifestyle. See Proverbs 1:10-19, especially verse 14.

12. Uplifting our human works alongside of the cross of Christ.

"**For if Abraham was justified by works, he has something to boast about, but not before God. For what does the Scripture say? 'Abraham believed God, and it was counted to him as righteousness.' Now to the one who works, his wages are not counted as a gift but as his due**" (Rom. 4:2-4 ESV). Also consider Isaiah 64:6 for further reflection and study.

"**For all have sinned and fall short of the glory of God, and are justified by his grace as a gift, through the redemption that is in Christ Jesus**" (Rom. 3:23-24 ESV).

On the meaninglessness of works of supererogation (special added works to prove one's righteous state), the converted Strict Franciscan, Francois Lambert of Avignon, quoted Luke 17:10. He used this verse in his testimony to show that our good works do not and cannot bring salvation, nor do they in some way increase grace:

"So you too, when you do all the things which are commanded you, say, 'We are unworthy slaves; we have done only that which we ought to have done'" (Luke 17:10 NASB).

13. Recycling Old Testament-type rituals:

The new covenant (Jesus's death on the cross) fulfilled the Old Testament demands of the Law:

"Do not think that I came to abolish the Law or the Prophets; I did not come to abolish but to fulfill. For truly I say to you, until heaven and earth pass away, not the smallest letter or stroke shall pass from the Law until all is accomplished" (Matt 5:17-18 NASB).

His sacrifice fulfilled the sacrificial role of all old covenant rituals. His death is sufficient and efficient. It supersedes the need for any and all other religious rituals for purification.

"For it is impossible for the blood of bulls and goats to take away sins. ... And by that will we have been sanctified through the offering of the body of Jesus Christ once for all. And every priest stands daily at his service, offering repeatedly the same sacrifices, which can never take away sins. But when Christ had offered for all time a single sacrifice for sins, he sat down at the right hand of God, waiting from that time until his enemies should be made a footstool for his feet. For by a single offering he has perfected for all time those who are being sanctified" (Heb. 10:4, 10-14 ESV). This same theme is also expanded in Hebrews 8:1-13 and 9:13-14.

"The next day he saw Jesus coming toward him, and said, 'Behold, the Lamb of God, who takes away the sin of the world!'" (John 1:29 ESV).

Jesus has done it all. His death on the cross has taken away the sin and sins of the world. We are left to bask in thanksgiving and praise of His name, humbly obeying His voice and following after Him.

14. Emphasizing the Sacraments above the cross of Christ:

Points 12 and 13 above both relate to the ineffectiveness and uselessness of religious rituals (even the Old Testament ones!) to cleanse from sin and provide grace and holiness. Rather grace is not earned or deserved, it is the gift of God.

"**For by grace you have been saved through faith. And this is not your own doing; it is the gift of God, not a result of works, so that no one may boast. For we are his workmanship, created in Christ Jesus for good works, which God prepared beforehand, that we should walk in them**" (Eph. 2:8-10 ESV).

Further, as in verse 10, by His grace, God has prepared good works for us, that we should walk in them. All glory goes to God. There is no glory to us for our human efforts. For this reason, we will one day—the entire world—sing to the glory of Christ alone.

"**And I heard every creature in heaven and on earth and under the earth and in the sea, and all that is in them, saying, 'To him who sits on the throne and to the Lamb be blessing and honor and glory and might forever and ever!' And the four living creatures said, 'Amen!' and the elders fell down and worshiped**'" (Rev. 5:13-14 ESV).

Faith alone saves, not physical Sacraments or any other exterior work:

"**Then he brought them out and said, 'Sirs, what must I do to be saved?' And they said, 'Believe in the Lord Jesus, and you will be saved, you and your household**'" (Acts 16:30-31 ESV).

Thew Philippian jailer was assured, "You will be saved!" What great assurance because of Jesus.

15. Granting indulgences or holy objects the ability to forgive sins:

This compromise of indulgences may be thought to be exemplified in Acts 19 where the Apostle Paul heals people through the use of physical objects:

"**And God was doing extraordinary miracles by the hands of Paul, so that even handkerchiefs or aprons that had touched his skin were carried away to the sick, and their diseases left them and the evil spirits came out of them**" (Acts 19:11-12 ESV).

Please note that these miracles of Paul did not include forgiveness of sins, nor salvation, nor even assurance of salvation. They were physical healings and release from demon possession. As discussed in Point 3 above, man is wont to cling to physical objects which are used like talismans and fetishes. These religious trinkets are so dangerous that Deuteronomy commanded them to be crushed and burned.

"**But thus you shall do to them: you shall tear down their altars, and smash their sacred pillars, and hew down their Asherim, and burn their graven images with fire**" (Deut. 7:5 NASB). For further consideration, see also Deuteronomy 7:25-26.

16. Giving priests the duty to grant absolution and forgiveness of sins:

"**And Jesus seeing their faith said to the paralytic, 'Son, your sins are forgiven.' But some of the scribes were sitting there and reasoning in their hearts, 'Why does this man speak that way? He is blaspheming; who can forgive sins but God alone?' Immediately Jesus, aware in His spirit that they were reasoning that way within themselves, said to them, 'Why are you reasoning about these things in your hearts? Which is easier, to say to the paralytic, "Your sins are forgiven"; or to say, "Get up, and pick up your pallet and walk"? But so that you may know that the Son of Man has authority on earth to forgive sins'—He said to the paralytic, 'I say to you, get up, pick up your pallet and go home**'" (Mark 2:5-11 NASB).

Were the scribes correct in stating, "**Who can forgive sins but God alone?**" Yes, and in that context, Jesus was and is God. Where in the Old Testament might the scribes have learned this principle that God and God alone has the authority to forgive sins?

"Moreover the LORD your God will circumcise your heart and the heart of your descendants, to love the LORD your God with all your heart and with all your soul, so that you may live" (Deut. 30:6 NASB).

"Rejoice, O nations, with His people; For He will avenge the blood of His servants, And will render vengeance on His adversaries, And will atone for His land and His people" (Deut 32:43 NASB). Also consider Micah 7:18 for further study on this topic.

The New Testament is abundantly clear that the authority to forgive sin resides only with Jesus:

"He has delivered us from the power of darkness and conveyed us into the kingdom of the Son of His love, in whom we have redemption through His blood, the forgiveness of sins'" (Col. 1:13-14 NKJV).

Jesus Christ alone died for our sins and can forgive sins. It is to Jesus that we are to confess our sins:

"If we confess our sins, he is faithful and just to forgive us our sins and to cleanse us from all unrighteousness. If we say we have not sinned, we make him a liar, and his word is not in us. My little children, I am writing these things to you so that you may not sin. But if anyone does sin, we have an advocate with the Father, Jesus Christ the righteous. He is the propitiation for our sins, and not for ours only but also for the sins of the whole world" (1 John 2:1-2 ESV). Also consider 1 John 1:5-8 on forgiveness of sins.

Jesus is our Lawyer or Advocate with the Father. Jesus is our Confessor. He alone is our Savior!

17. Shifting from a focus from the gospel of Christ to a focus on a particular church or church leader:

"For I decided to know nothing among you except Jesus Christ and him crucified" (1 Cor. 2:2 ESV).

"I am astonished that you are so quickly deserting him who called you in the grace of Christ and are turning to a different gospel—not that there is another one, but there are some who trouble you and want to distort the gospel of Christ" (Gal. 1:6-7 ESV). Also consider what Paul wrote in Galatians 5:11 on this topic.

"Therefore everyone who hears these words of Mine and acts on them, may be compared to a wise man who built his house on the rock. And the rain fell, and the floods came, and the winds blew and slammed against that house; and yet it did not fall, for it had been founded on the rock. Everyone who hears these words of Mine and does not act on them, will be like a foolish man who built his house on the sand. The rain fell, and the floods came, and the winds blew and slammed against that house; and it fell—and great was its fall" (Matt. 7:24-27 NASB).

We must constantly redirect our faith and our hearts to the words of Jesus and His cross. Any movement away from that focus is dangerous to our faith.

18. Making assurance of salvation the first cardinal sin, the sin of pride:

More than most other doctrines, anathematizing assurance of salvation was and is the blood-soaked thread that connects historical eras and amalgamates heretics of multiples names and cultures. In the second millennium Thomas Aquinas wrote of assurance of salvation as the "vainglory of the heretics." In the first millennium, Pope Gregory I divided sin into two categories, quite without any biblical authority to do so: the mortal sins (outward sins, such as adultery and murder) and the cardinal sins (inward sins, such as coveting and pride). The chief cardinal sin for Gregory was the sin of pride. Interpretation, "You think that you know that you are going to heaven? Why that's the sin of pride—You can't know that!" Pride in the Catholic catalog of sins is their first, highest, and primary sin.[11] Hence, for trained Catholics, heretics in their vainglory fall prey to the highest of all possible sins, the

[11] Yes, Aquinas in his Summa (Second Part of the Second Part) did argue that love was the greatest good, and therefore the lack of love—for the Pope and his church—was the greatest evil, to the same end.

sin of pride. **"Their blood is upon them"** (Lev. 20:11 ESV). This same teaching is repeated in Leviticus 20:12, 13, 16, and 27. Hence, it is the heretics own fault if he is burned alive, since "his blood is upon him."

On the other hand, here are some comforting verses from the New Testament teaching assurance of salvation in Jesus Christ:

"Therefore, since we have been justified by faith, we have peace with God through our Lord Jesus Christ. Through him we have also obtained access by faith into this grace in which we stand, and we rejoice in hope of the glory of God" (Rom. 5:1-2 ESV).

"There is therefore now no condemnation to those who are in Christ Jesus, who do not walk according to the flesh, but according to the Spirit"
(Rom. 8:1 NKJV).

"Truly, truly, I say to you, he who hears My word, and believes Him who sent Me, has eternal life, and does not come into judgment, but has passed out of death into life" (John 5:24 NASB).

"And this is the testimony: that God has given us eternal life, and this life is in His Son. He who has the Son has life; he who does not have the Son of God does not have life. These things I have written to you who believe in the name of the Son of God, that you may know that you have eternal life, and that you may continue to believe in the name of the Son of God" (1 John 5:11-13 NKJV).

The New Testament not only offers assurance of salvation by grace through faith in Jesus Christ, but it also offers assurance of perseverance by that same grace.

Roman Catholicism: An Introduction and Bible Study

A Review of the New Testament Gospel

The New Testament contains several passages that provide succinct enumerations of the gospel and how it is meant to be received. It is helpful to meditate on these Scriptures.

1. What is the gospel?

   From the lips of Jesus after His resurrection: "**Then He said to them, 'Thus it is written, and thus it was necessary for the Christ to suffer and to rise from the dead the third day, and that repentance and remission of sins should be preached in His name to all nations, beginning at Jerusalem**'" (Luke 24:46-47 NKJV).

   From the pen of the Apostle Paul: "**Now I would remind you, brothers, of the gospel I preached to you, which you received, in which you stand, and by which you are being saved, if you hold fast to the word I preached to you—unless you believed in vain. For I delivered to you as of first importance what I also received: that Christ died for our sins in accordance with the Scriptures, that he was buried, that he was raised on the third day in accordance with the Scriptures, and that he appeared to Cephas, then to the twelve**" (1 Cor. 15:1-5 ESV).

2. How is the gospel received?

   "**And when there had been much dispute, Peter rose up and said to them: 'Men and brethren, you know that a good while ago God chose among us, that by my mouth the Gentiles should hear the word of the gospel and believe. So God, who knows the heart, acknowledged them by giving them the Holy Spirit, just as He did to us, and made no distinction between us and them, purifying their hearts by faith. Now therefore, why do you test God by putting a yoke on the neck of the disciples which neither our fathers nor we were able to bear? But we believe that through the grace of the Lord Jesus Christ we shall be saved in the same manner as they**'" (Acts 15:7-11 NKJV).

Salvation begins with a verbal witness, "**by my mouth the Gentiles should hear**." What was the message that they heard? It was the gospel, "**the word of the gospel**." They received that gospel by believing (hence faith alone), "**and believe**." These several elements explained all that was necessary for the "**purifying of their hearts by faith**." The entire process was all because of the "**grace of the Lord Jesus**" (hence grace alone, without the addition of any works). In fact, Peter stated that the addition of works to salvation was "**putting a yoke on the neck of the disciples which neither our fathers nor we were able to bear**." Peter was seeking to protect the church in Jerusalem from adding works to the free gift of salvation in Jesus Christ. These same principles are found in Romans 3:19-26.

Consider in this light the humble simplicity of the words Paul and Silas shared in Acts 16: "**And he brought them out and said, 'Sirs, what must I do to be saved?' So they said, 'Believe on the Lord Jesus Christ, and you will be saved, you and your household**'" (Acts 16:30-31 NKJV).

Receiving the gospel is by grace alone and through faith alone. There is no indication of the need for the reception of water on the head or a host on the tongue. The Holy Spirit works through His words to do salvific surgery on the hearts and souls of men. Likewise, Jesus explained the amazing spiritual property of His words to give life: "**It is the Spirit who gives life; the flesh profits nothing. The words that I speak to you are spirit, and they are life**" (John 6:63 NKJV).

Believing the words of Jesus about His Father seals our salvation: "**Truly, truly, I say to you, whoever hears my word and believes him who sent me has eternal life. He does not come into judgment, but has passed from death to life**" (John 5:24 ESV). Isn't God gracious to us in Christ Jesus?

John summarized the reason that he wrote his biography of Jesus in this way: "**Now Jesus did many other signs in the presence of the disciples, which are not written in this book; but these are written so that you may believe that Jesus is the Christ, the Son of God, and that by believing you may have life in his name**" (John 20:30-31 ESV).

Along with this great salvation, we end with a final warning from Scripture:

> **"For I testify to everyone who hears the words of the prophecy of this book: If anyone adds to these things, God will add to him the plagues that are written in this book; and if anyone takes away from the words of the book of this prophecy, God shall take away his part from the Book of Life, from the holy city, and from the things which are written in this book**" (Rev. 22:18-19 NKJV).

Made in the USA
Monee, IL
08 March 2026

45696788R00017